T5-ANY-609

# Old MacDonald Has a Farm

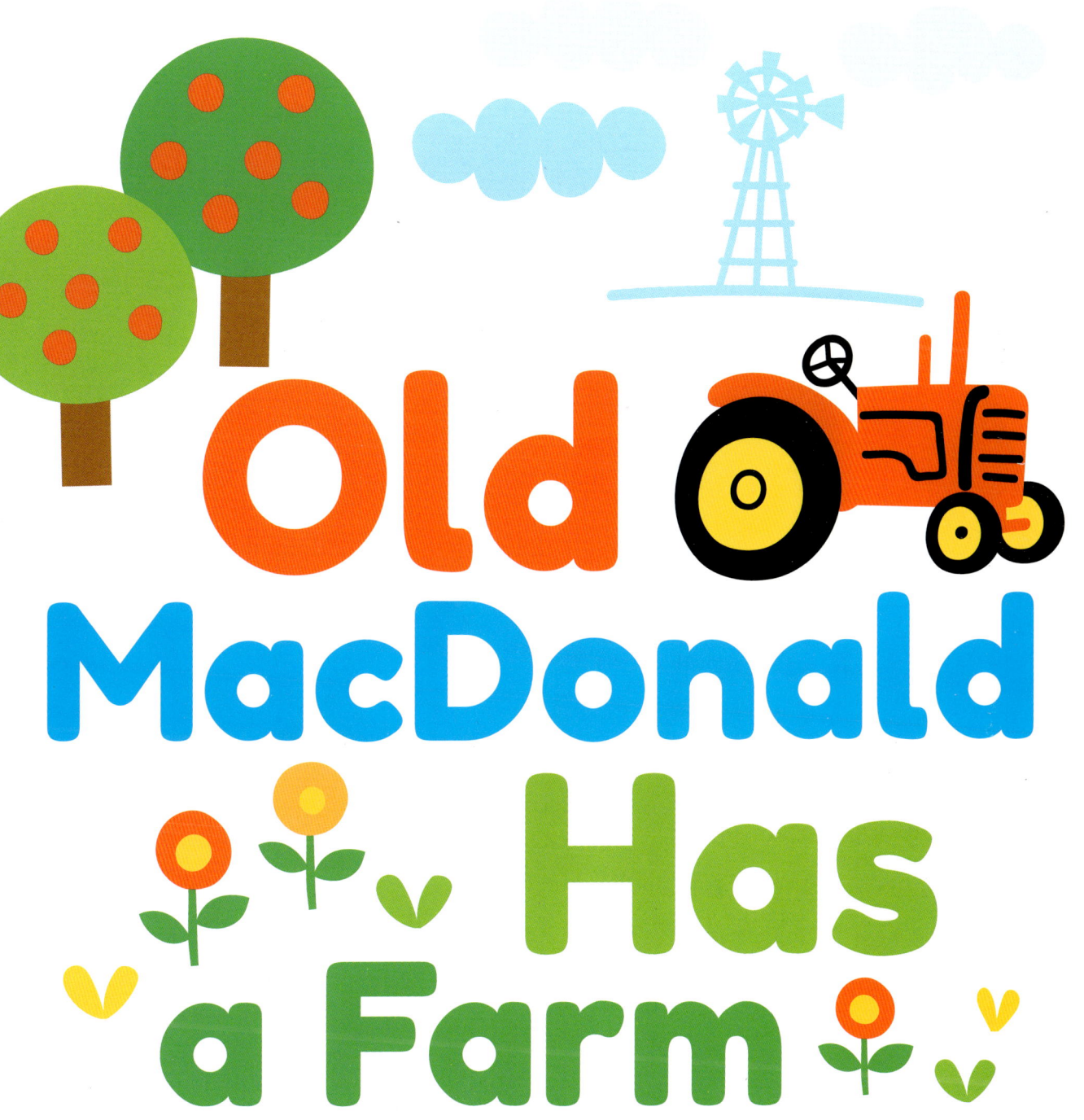

By Leslie Falconer and Chris Lensch

First published by Experience Early Learning Company
7243 Scotchwood Lane, Grawn, Michigan 49637 USA

Copyright © 2019 by Experience Early Learning Co.
Manufactured in No.8, Yin Li Street, Tian He District, Guangzhou, Guangdong, China
by Sun Fly Printing Limited
2rd Printing 12/2021

ISBN: 978-1-937954-57-4
Visit us at www.ExperienceEarlyLearning.com

# Old MacDonald has a farm.

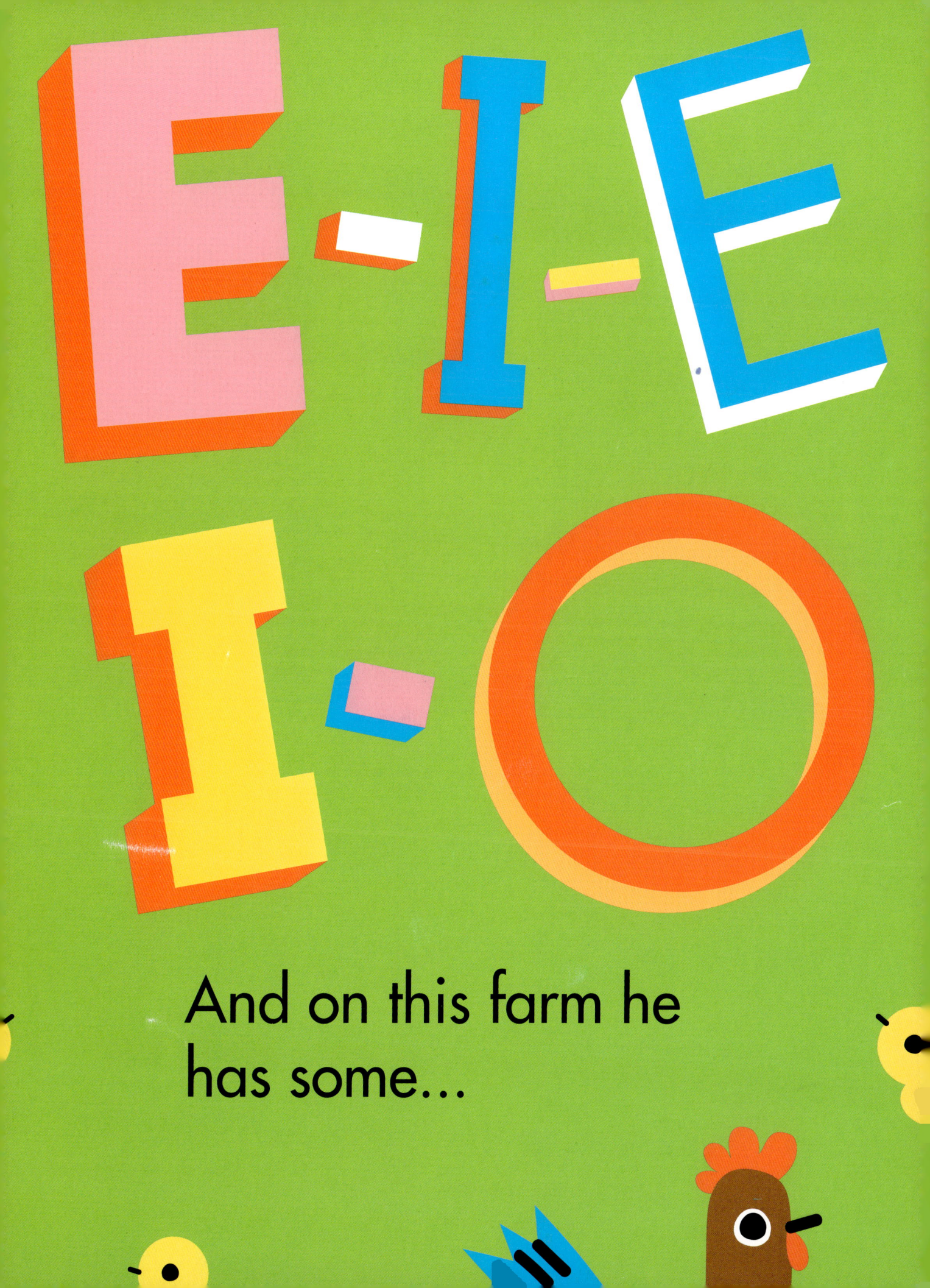

# E-I-E
# I-O

And on this farm he has some...

# Chicks!

E-I-E-I-O

With a peep-peep here.

And a peep-peep there.

Here a peep.

There a peep.

Everywhere a peep-peep.

Old MacDonald has a farm.
E-I-E-I-O

# Old MacDonald has a farm.

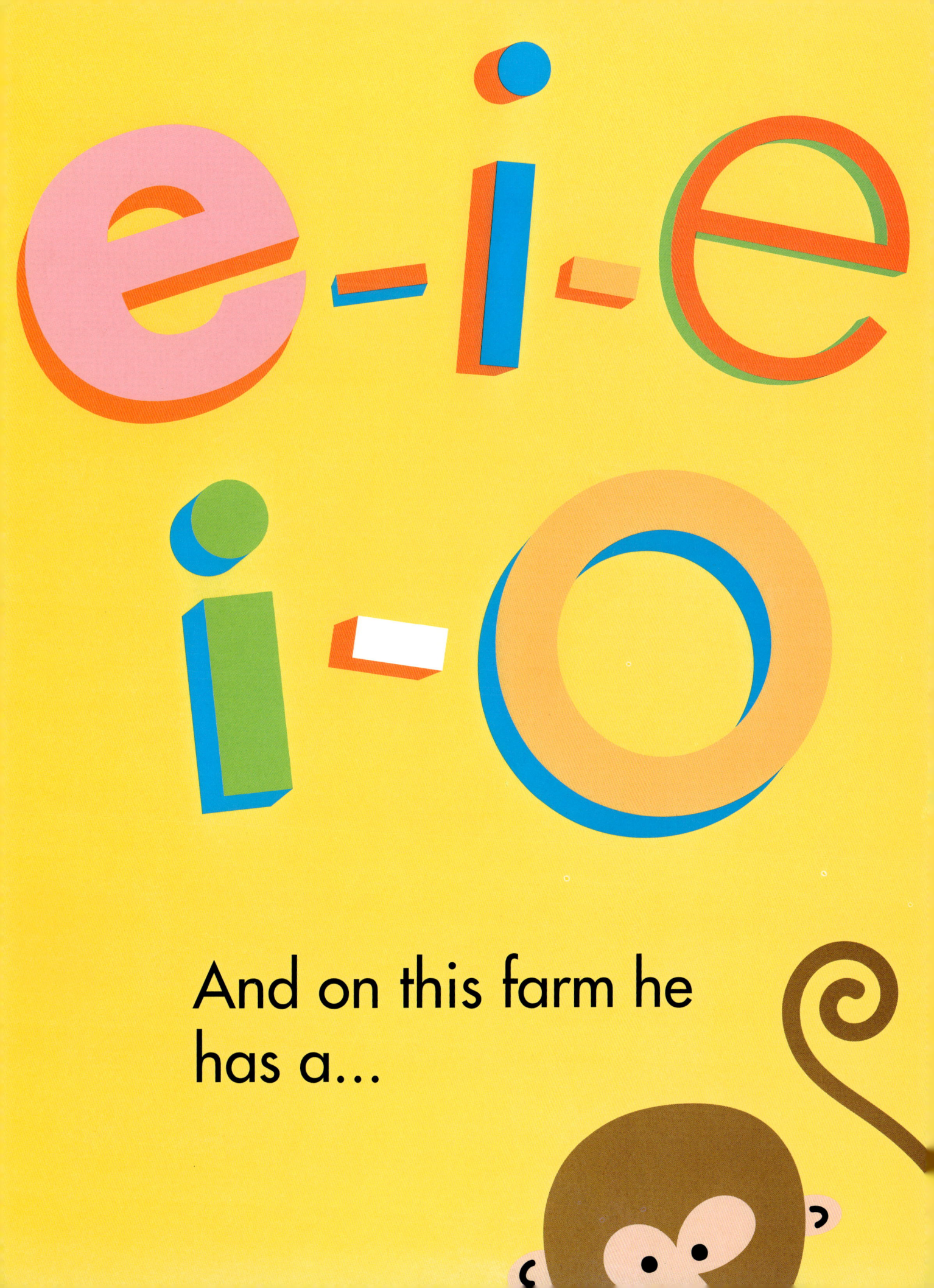

# e-i-e
# i-o

And on this farm he has a...

Monkey. A monkey?

It's okay. You can stay.

# Cow!

E-I-E-I-O

E-I-E

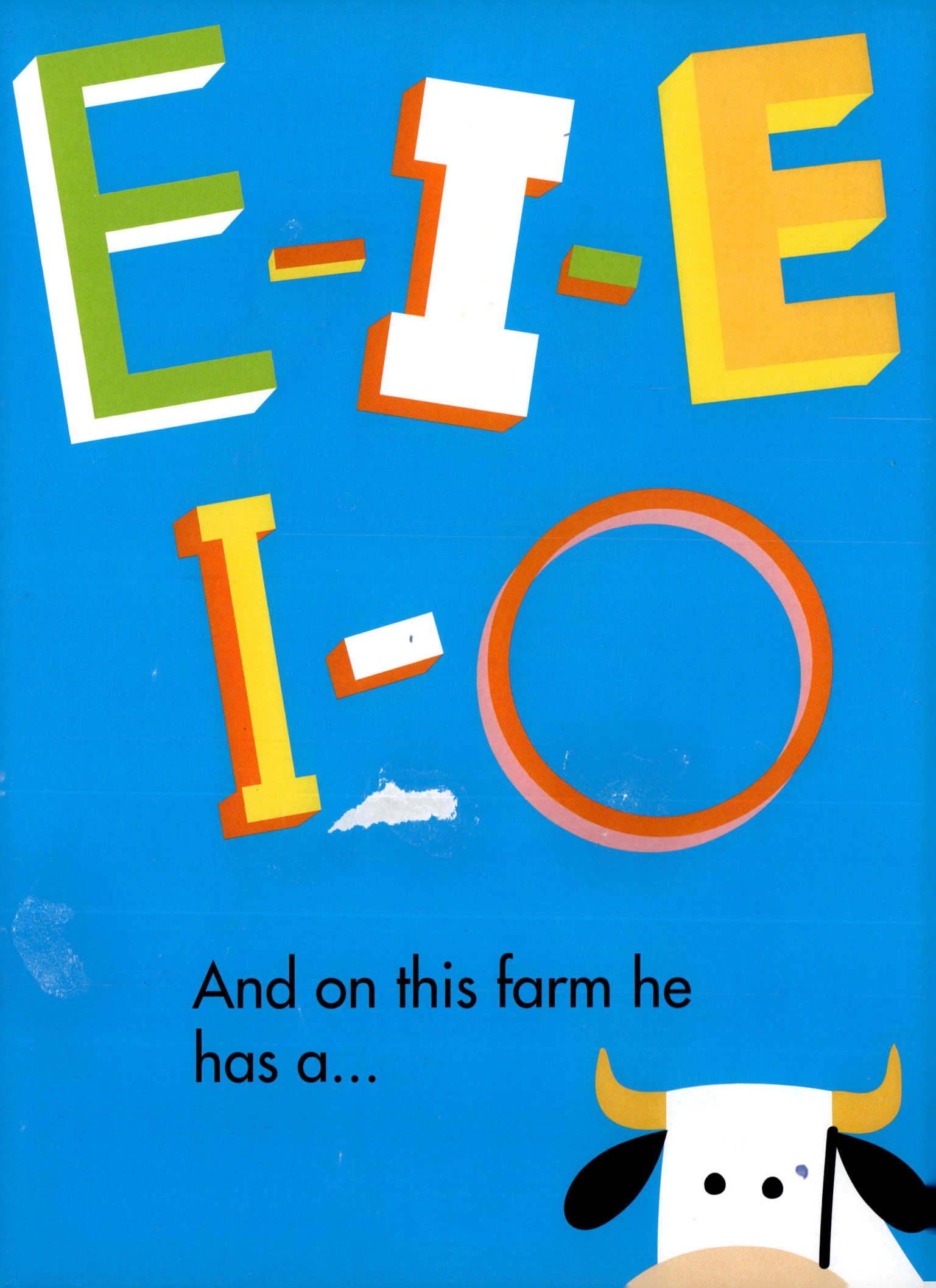

I-O

And on this farm he has a...

Old MacDonald has a farm.

With an ooo-ooo here.

And an ooo-ooo there.

Here an ooo.

There an ooo.

Everywhere an ooo-ooo.

Old MacDonald has a farm.
Where everyone belongs.

With a moo-moo here.

And a moo-moo there.

Here a moo.

There a moo.

Everywhere a moo-moo.

Old MacDonald has a farm.
E-I-E-I-O

# Old MacDonald has a farm.

# e-i-e
# i-o

And on this farm he has a...

# Giraffe. A giraffe?

It's okay. You can stay.

With a clip-clop here.

Here a clip.

And a clip-clop there.

There a clop.

Everywhere a clip-clop.

Old MacDonald has a farm.
Where everyone belongs.

# Old MacDonald has a farm.

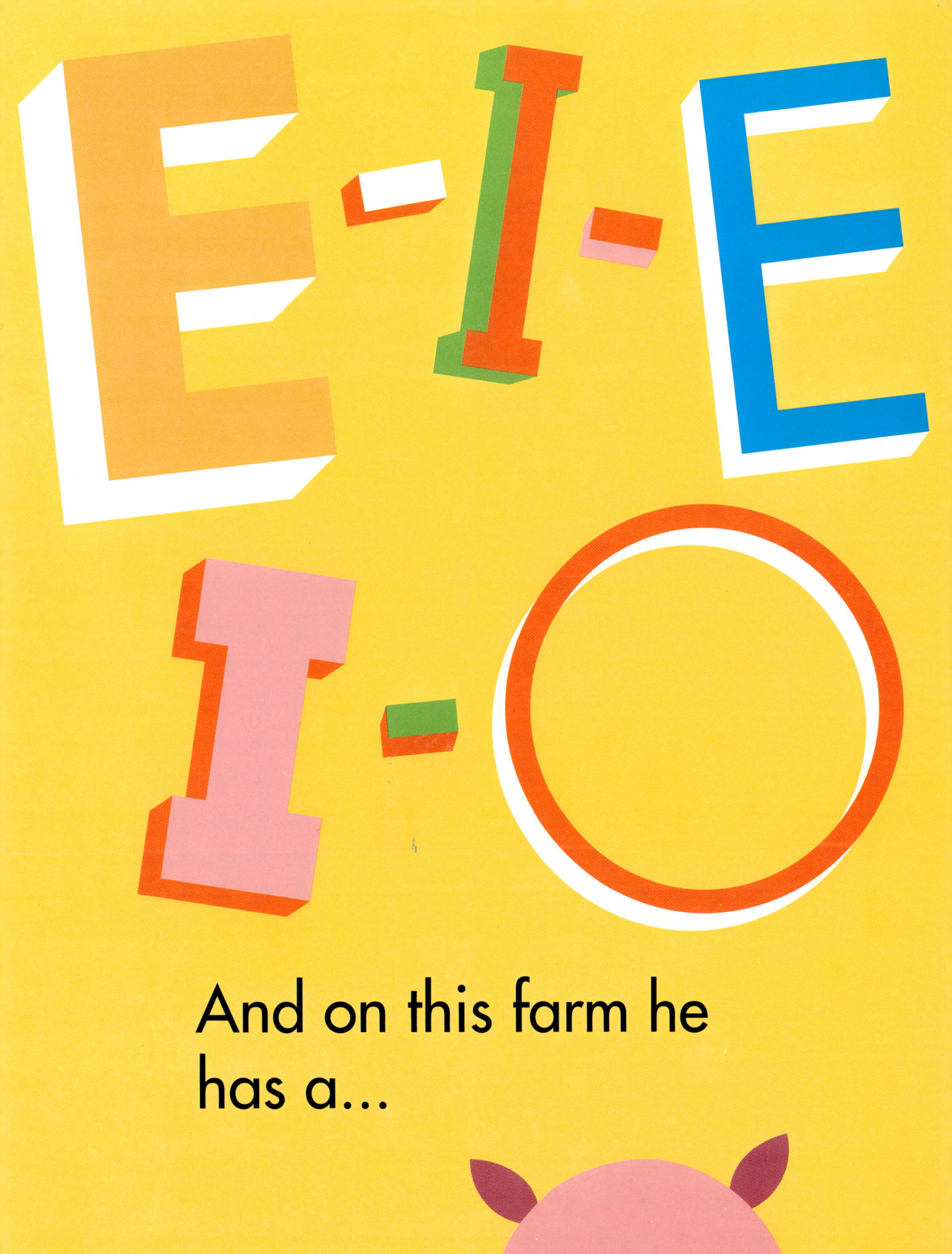

E-I-E
I-O

And on this farm he has a...

# Pig!

E-I-E-I-O

With an oink-oink here.

And an oink-oink there.

Here an oink.

There an oink.

Everywhere an oink-oink.

Old MacDonald has a farm.
E-I-E-I-O

# Old MacDonald has a farm.

e-i-e-i

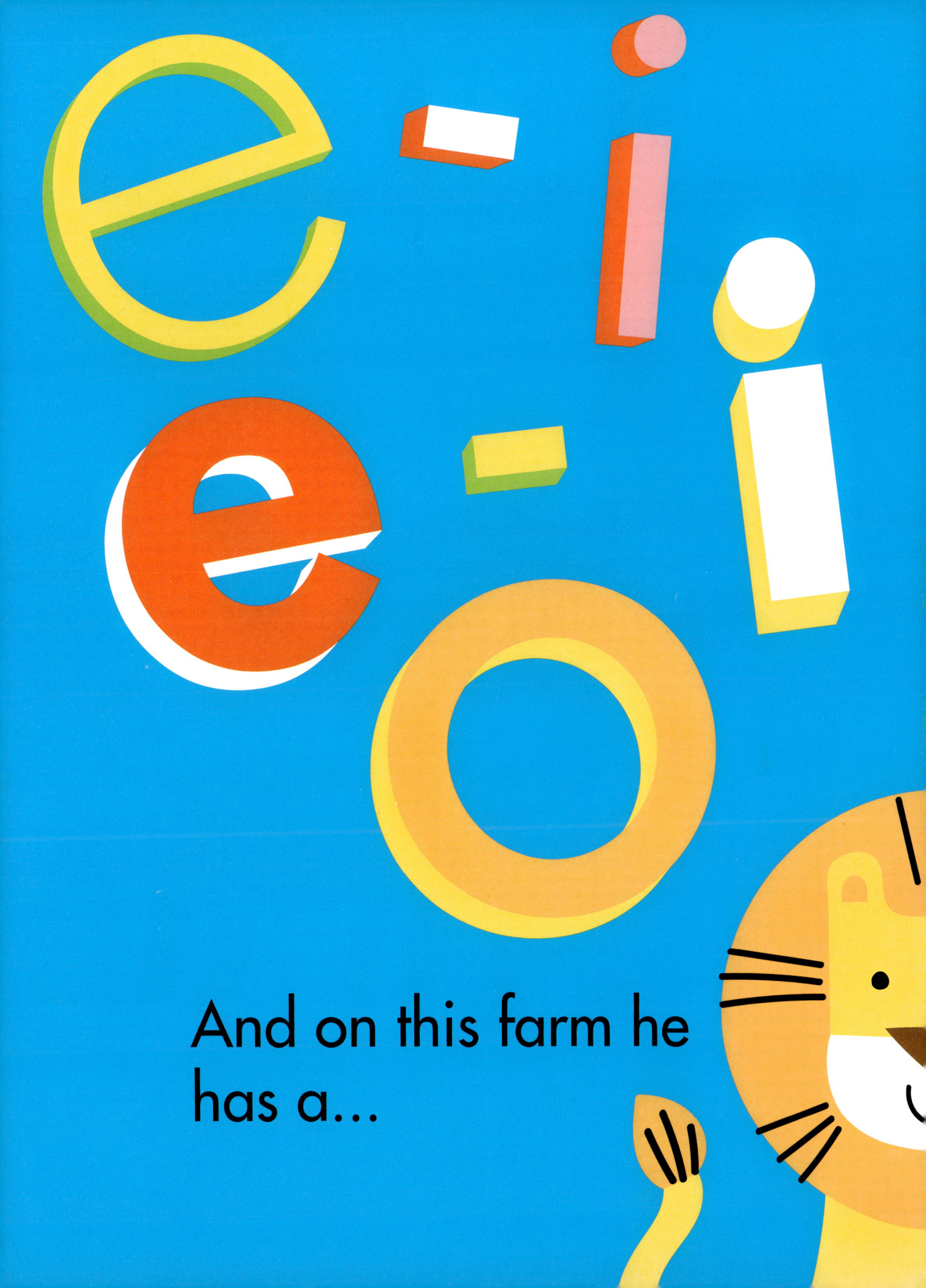

e-o-i

And on this farm he has a...

Lion. A lion?

It's okay. You can stay.

With a roar-roar here.

And a roar-roar there.

Here a roar.

There a roar.

Everywhere a roar-roar.

Old MacDonald has a farm.

Where everyone belongs.

The end